I Have to Go Back to 1994 and Kill a Girl

I Have to
Go Back to 1994
and Kill a Girl

▼▼▼▼▼▼▼

poems by
Karyna McGlynn

WINNER OF THE 2008
KATHRYN A. MORTON PRIZE IN POETRY
SELECTED BY LYNN EMANUEL

Sarabande S📖 Books
LOUISVILLE, KENTUCKY

No part of this book may be reproduced without written permission of the publisher. Please direct inquiries to:

Managing Editor
Sarabande Books, Inc.
2234 Dundee Road, Suite 200
Louisville, KY 40205

Library of Congress Cataloging-in-Publication Data

McGlynn, Karyna.
    I have to go back to 1994 and kill a girl : poems / by Karyna McGlynn ; selected by Lynn Emanuel for Sarabande Books. — 1st ed.
        p.   cm.
    ISBN 978-1-932511-76-5 (pbk. : alk. paper)
    I. Emanuel, Lynn, 1949- II. Title.
    PS3613.C486I3 2009
    811'.6—dc22   2009000926

ISBN-13: 978-1-932511-76-5

Cover art: Miranda Lehman

Cover and text design by Charles Casey Martin

Manufactured in Canada
This book is printed on acid-free paper.

Sarabande Books is a nonprofit literary organization.

The Kentucky Arts Council, the state arts agency, supports Sarabande Books with state tax dollars and federal funding from the National Endowment for the Arts.

ENVIRONMENTAL BENEFITS STATEMENT
Sarabande Books saved the following resources by printing the pages of this book on chlorine free paper made with 100% postconsumer waste.

TREES	WATER	ENERGY	SOLID WASTE	GREENHOUSE GASES
18	6,563	12	843	1,561
FULLY GROWN	GALLONS	MILLION BTUs	POUNDS	POUNDS

Calculations based on research by Environmental Defense and the Paper Task Force. Manufactured at Friesens Corporation.

Green publication made possible by a donation from Linda E. Beattie in honor of Marion Kingston Stocking.

for Nell G. (1923–2006), thanks for the pennies

CONTENTS

ii. Visitant

iii. Revenant

ACKNOWLEDGMENTS

Many thanks to the editors of the journals in which these poems first appeared, sometimes in earlier forms:

42opus: "Erin with the Feathered Hair."

Another Chicago Magazine: "The Fox Had no Face the Loggermen Said," "He Also Outside, a Cold Paisley," "Lucifer Who Put This Moment in a Clear Block of Gelatin."

Coconut: "Not that I'm Neuter Exactly Said the Child in the Yard."

The Concher: "It Wasn't Phenomenal, She Followed the Phone Poles Up & Up."

Copper Nickel: "When I Came to There Was a Pearl and a Fish Hook."

Diode: "I Want to Introduce Myself, Not Quite Human," "La Parc Darque But You Can Only Magnify It," "The Thing in the Middle Which Has No Corner."

Forklift, Ohio: "In a Landscape the Color of Bleached Limes," "Sometime in the Night a Naked Man Passes."

GlitterPony: "I Found Pennies on My Skin, I Put Them There."

Horse Less Review: "This Grand Conversation Was Under the Rose," "Before Anything Happened the House Had No Skeleton."

La Petite Zine: "At the Far End of the Room Buzzed with 40 Tiny Fans," ". . . & the Southern Cross Slid Below the Belt."

Octopus: "They Shared Her on a Chicken White Sheet," "I Have to Go Back to 1994 and Kill a Girl," "To Step Off the El's Chlamydeous Tongue," "Somebody Shook Me: Wake Up It's Raining Oil."

Oleander Review: "The Poem with Its Teeth Caught In the Carpet," "We Both Dyed with Feria Starlet, I Couldn't Dispossess a Girl."

Past Simple: "Ok, but you haven't seen the last of me."

Pebble Lake Review: "Post-Nuptials: The Wedding Party Floated Away on an Iceberg."

POOL: "Glass Backlog," "Where There Should Be a Plant Stand, There Isn't," "The Woods Are Calling but I Go to a Sleepover."

Siren: "Square in the Gut of Lovemaking Lessons," "To Be Curled in the Snail Light of Your Heathen," "Oh, You Really Don't Want to Go into the Library," "I Want to Tell Her I Won't Need Calculus, I Want to Warn Her."

Spork: "I Show Up Twelve Years Late for Curfew."

Subtropics: "A Girl Bellycrawls into My Room in Weeds," "Postcoital Pippi."

Typo Magazine: "Would You Like Me to Walk Your Baby?" "A Door Left Open at the Place I Didn't Rent."

Verse Daily: "Before Anything Happened the House Had No Skeleton."

"Would You Like Me to Walk Your Baby?" later appeared in the *2006 Best of the Net* anthology.

Some of the poems in this manuscript also appear in a chapbook, *Scorpionica* (New Michigan Press, 2007).

I am deeply indebted to my family for letting me pursue something so utterly unrealistic for so long, and to the University of Michigan MFA program and Helen Zell for their unparalleled and continuing generosity.

I also wish to extend thanks to Thomas Lynch for the use of his Irish cottage where many of the poems were first conceived (and also for the headstone with my name on it!); to Miranda Lehman for the use of one of her lovely photos, which you should check out more of at http://ghostinthewoods.com; to the lovely folks at Squaw Valley in 2006 who encouraged many of these poems in their infancy: Dean Young, C. D. Wright, Sharon Olds, Harryette Mullen and Bob Hass; to Tony Hoagland, who's unaware of the myriad ways he's helped me; to Lynn Emanuel for her amazing introduction, and to Sarah, Nickole, Kirby, Jen, and Meg at Sarabande for making this book happen.

Finally, for friendship, support and editorial insight, I wish to thank: Chris Adams, Sharon Cumberland and the Seattle U. English Dept., Bruce Covey, Peter Ho Davies, Linda Gregerson, Marie Howe, Cyan James, Anna Journey, Megan Levad, Emily Mahan, Ray McDaniel, Khaled Mattawa, Ander Monson, Simone Muench, Tim Kneedler, Beau Paul, Adam Rubinstein, Nate Slawson, Jon Sterk, Susan B. A. Somers-Willett and especially Adam Theriault whose empathy and big-picture thinking I can't imagine living without.

FOREWORD

What do we mean by "innovative"? This question, which haunts current American poetry, is at the forefront of the experience of reading Karyna McGlynn's extraordinary first book *I Have to Go Back to 1994 and Kill A Girl*. Upon reading it, I am reminded of early encounters with the conceptual artists of the 1980s: Cindy Sherman's photographs, the slogans on Jenny Holzer's tombstones, "Abuse of power comes as no surprise," and the appropriation art of Sherrie Levine. One was drawn to all these works because of their vague (or in Levine's case, absolute) familiarity, a familiarity that turned to quicksand the longer one looked.

and none could be	superimposed
anyway you	could only spot
its topside with 1	eye closed, 1
eye spotting	itself in another
life more fully	exposed

—"...la Parc Darque but You Can Only Magnify It"

I Have to Go Back to 1994 and Kill a Girl is also haunted by the question: Are these poems autobiographical? Do they propose several possible, even alternative lives? This book takes liberties with our expectations of the acceptable pace and manner of disclosure in a book of poems. Like Sherman or Levine, McGlynn creates a world that seems (almost) familiar, a world that momentarily hoodwinks and seduces us into the sleep of our usual expectations. As a literary antecedent, *I Have to Go Back to 1994 and Kill a Girl* gestures to Robert Lowell's cagey, slippery, (and often overlooked) formulation of his Confessionalism, "A reader should feel he is getting the real Robert Lowell." Ultimately, this is not a book that hews poetry out of a sense of getting the real anything. Nevertheless, what makes it so crafty is that it uses the language and the style we have come to associate with the real and authentic "self"—trauma, violation, sexuality—to subvert the expected self and its confessions. *I Have to Go Back to 1994 and Kill a Girl* is a kind of "appropriation autobiography," it produces the feeling that we know something, have read it before, or even experienced it ourselves; it has the tang of familiarity. It is familiar. And then suddenly, ruthlessly, it is not.

The title contains the method and subject of the book. The past must be killed. There is an uncompromising, dazzling cold-heartedness to this ambition. On the cover we read the title announcing the intention of murder. When we open the book and are confronted with the section titles—"Planchette," "Visitant," "Revenant"—we are in a world where the past is already dead. The murder has occurred, and there is nothing left but phantoms. Not only has the central action of this book, the murder, already taken place, but it happened offstage. This is one example of the skill with which McGlynn manipulates time. It is also an example of the skill with which McGlynn tampers with our expectation of disclosure. She does this within the frame of a single poem. She does it by subtly, brilliantly, manipulating the book's structure and architecture. A reader will learn nothing of the murderer or the victim until well into the book's third and final section, which contains the title poem.

I Have to Go Back to 1994 and Kill a Girl is a remarkable book. It is innovative, original, unprecedented and, at the same time, its originality and innovation are predicated on a passionate, even obsessive, relationship with the past. There is a playfulness in this work that is darkly ironic. To be a reader of *I Have to Go Back to 1994 and Kill a Girl* is to be a time traveler. Yet, no matter which life, body, or landscape one lands in, all exist on a shared bedrock of violence and suffering, albeit one presided over by a glittering imagination:

> they rolled a barrelful of something muffled
> down the back of a mountain...

there were spiders hatching inside her mattress
we said that's not what's hatching

she opened her mouth to call her father inside
a small pile of salt fell out.

—"The Fox Had No Face the Loggermen Said"

—Lynn Emanuel

Killing you is killing myself. But, you know, I'm pretty tired of both of us.
—*The Lady from Shanghai*, Dir. Orson Welles, 1947

"Ok, but you haven't seen the last of me"

I wake up somewhere in Ohio. Or, that's how it smells—

There's a phone in my hand. I'm thirty years old.
No, the phone is thirty years old. Its memory's been erased.

I'm naked but for one of those hollowed scarves.
It keeps peeling off like a seedpod.

I'm afraid my sense will fall out,
get lost in the snow and make more of me.

Up ahead, I think, *there's a covered bridge.*

I remember her eyes, but not her name:
two busts of dead composers, ivory in very cold water.

Her name touches my lungs like the edge of a plate. Hypothermia.
Sault Ste. Marie up ahead. I climb a tree and look into the future.

A hope chest full of nuts, rats in a burrow. Her body banked against mine,
an obsolete piece of machinery I keep for some reason:

such hair and nails, an eiderdown coat—

PLANCHETTE

You may not realize that you are moving the message
indicator, but you are.

Before Anything Happened the House Had No Skeleton

the termites had deboned the thing
it was clean there was no saving it

in one bedroom a dresser with blue drawers
its peg-legs rested on pure membrane

a girl just stood in her underwear
ran the tips of her fingers over her ribs

thought *greyhound* no one knew no explaining
why she didn't fall through the floor

the kids were drinking beer in the yard
the tetherball rope caught one girl's throat

her mother's face obscured
behind the porch screen the mesquite shadow

no one could make her out
her feet rested on hot sashes of dust

the sounds on the television were far away
as that big caliche mound looked like a waving man

the president got shot
the boards stayed together for another three days

it was a matter of apathy or swelling
or everyone was too hot to move

Not that I'm Neuter Exactly Said the Child in the Yard

I have a straight line drawn down here
                        more I'm neural
it says I step out from the green light
            of the townhouse
that trussed the bed, the TV & the toilet
                        I step outside
into the yard which is enclosed by a wall
            that's for the best
b/c my line and my 2 lines are showing
                        but my hair I say
is more of a concept there is a whiter
            a smaller door up
above the bin & the grating & my 2 eyes
                        empty as quarters
rubbed smooth my body is only a wall
            failing but a light
and a shadow which makes something of
                        the shape a child
draws an evergreen it's coming down
            over me & inside
the channels go round & round where
                        someone's thumb
was stuck to a dial & sliced from the joint

A Red Tricycle in the Belly of the Pool

the live oak over the nursery got a disease
they could only save one limb
it wasn't surprising; it wasn't that kind of nursery

a girl rode her red tricycle around the bottom of the pool
the pool had no water; it hadn't rained

the girl kept smelling her hand
it smelled like honeywheat, or the inside of a girl's panties

someone said, race you
she nodded okay and pedaled like hell
after three laps no one had passed her

she looked over her shoulder, lost her balance
ripped her hands & knees on the blue concrete

the one limb on the live oak curved like a question
would she need stitches again

there was already ink under her skin & iodine on her tongue
or was it the other way around

she could see black thread bunching
sewing centipedes under her skin

her throat burned and she couldn't move her legs
it wasn't a tricycle
it was something she couldn't get her foot out from under

she hated to stop or lose her shoe and, I'm sorry
the pool was full of water

I Want to Introduce Myself, Not Quite Human

Before any conclusion, he's a boy
up & down some private pier—
to cluster & shock,
from the gas-shallows:
up the leg of his shorts
alchemical property & resort to
I want to prevent—
to keep bad words from coming into
his possession? How to excise with a volt
from his tremendous frame
Act-O tongued precision
I mean the cell words which will
yoke every mote of him to revolt—
this bleached body: his
form caught deep

in bleached jean shorts, running
Before my girlhood's even begun
I wave an eel's embodied 'hello'
from that shy, bilious space
I borrow every conceivable
medieval remedy. There is so much
What sort of entity must I inhabit
the terrible acumen of
these toxic suggestions
of reference? With an X-
I clean him of ringleaders—
invisibly
spirit slaking from
damp shorts on a dock, my elver
in the gut of a roller

Oh, You Really Don't Want to Go Into the Library

you have no future there

        this violet in pieces in John Maynard Keynes
        this pressed columbine in Joseph Conrad
        you practice on your own hand

        (a joystick & a bag of fertilizer)

what is this: some joke?

        the bull's testicles draped inside the book
        two grenades
        the tribal woman's breasts hung on the page
        brown eggs in a mesh bag

        (death & sex tickle the same damn spot)

get out get out get out

        you push this trolley toward the far end
        it is walleyed, wheel askew
        it keeps asking for the exit

        if you ask dewey to wrap you in his black coat
        he will

        (he'll lay you low & cover you completely)

Where There Should Be a Plant Stand, There Isn't

I hear people talking in the kitchen, but there's no way
to get to them; they've had three drinks too many.

The worst is my bedroom, which has been roped off
with yellow police tape. They've pulled up the carpet.

I think *someone's been here—a smoker,*
trying to bypass the now-defunct security system.

Through my window I see my sister step from her car.
She plans to confront me about the thing she can't yet know.

I slip back through the shotgun rooms, and once again
enter my mother's with its unheated waterbed.

In the left-hand drawer of her vanity, I know I can find
her expired pregnancy test with its indelible blue lines.

But, perhaps, like everything else, these are mutable details.
Shouting somewhere in the house now and I have to hurry.

If I take it out now, I might kill myself. If I leave it
I won't remember what I came here to do.

Amanda Hopper's House

It was a farmhouse for killing,
        the kind I saw in the paper above a row of senior portraits:

girls found in the basement.
        Frosted eye-shadow, bangs like birds' nests.

Girls I saw and said to myself:
        good. they deserve it.

"The stupid *sluts*" sit on my tongue.
        I swallow, but the stupid sluts stick there like chicken bones.

Like Amanda's older sister Gloria,
        splayed across the hood of her boyfriend's Chevy Nova.

From the breakfast table
        we watch him open her dry skinny legs and press

his belt buckle into her denim crotch.
        It's 9 a.m. and they chew grape gum.

We follow the unfurling snail silhouettes of their French kisses
        as Mrs. Hopper looks out, wary, from behind

the newspaper headline: *Body of Missing Teen Found in Family Shed.*
　　　She fishes in her pink robe for a pack of cigarettes,

places a menthol between her feathering lips,
　　　flicks her lighter, picks her cuticle,

tells us out the corner of her mouth
　　　to stop gaping and eat our fucking Lucky Charms.

In a Landscape the Color of Bleached Limes

why the animal stretched its neck is beyond me

it wasn't a black alpaca
it had eyes as Chinese stars but bigger

it had no chin or ears
it was peering at the sky and then at me

someone cut the frames where it moved

are you trying to drown yourself I said
it hasn't rained in a week

it said you don't remember but you have no mouth

true enough
I sat in a taxi which drove straight to the airport

I shut my mouth sour with nails
it's the only place I paid the driver to go

His Cancer Had Calves Milked of Magnesium

but pretend there were
or what to bring him
chicken thin his legs
like his middle name
the fact of him snapped
diffuse in the flume
of my childhood where
when I am pulling up
mine like white gasoline
contrary honey to what
your damned dignity is not

these options
for dinner
in the sheet
was Patrick
down infinite
our duplex
guilt crops
my bluejeans
in the ear
you were & will be
so important

like which wood
Kentucky fried
remember things
nothing can change
younger than myself
seamed inside the lip
up & he steps down
his mind pores over
in the dream he says:
why not pretend
as your plumb?

This Grand Conversation Was Under the Rose

the rose hung on a fishhook
from the creel in her glove
she flicked the thing like rapist bait

she leaned against her blind Clydesdale
in a blind alley her tongue tripped
weimaresque dietrich type dietrich type

like a man w/ top hat and tails
she flexed her leathered fist *you know*
she said *tonight is coming on all virulent*

and it was the grass was sodden
in some beetleshell ink & turtlewax gas
you know the horse snorted

you know said the half-clown
who crouched below her on a soapbox
I haven't even finished my make up

her tongue made a sound
like a whip culled of freshwater eel
she tightened the leash on her rose

Sometime in the Night a Naked Man Passes

the foot of my bed in a beekeeper's mask
con permiso, he says, they like to lay eggs in my face
where are you going, I say
the women in my life, he says, stroking the bedpost
who let you in, I say
I watch for expressions in his belly, his cock
both curve out, back in, his even breathing
a bee enters my open window & lands on his thumb
I'm sorry, he says, I was just leaving
where were you going, I say
to finish what they started, he says

The Poem with Its Teeth Caught In the Carpet

makes me afraid to move
         for the fffff of felt sounds
as I will wake the dog   against basically bone
         and it will lick a part of me
that I ever attempted   not yet called into being
         this flipflop & landed inside
god I'm a gangly thing   my mouth—lord it's dark
         on my belly & my shorts
& my yarn arm tongue   pulled around my knees
         I've left the fishsticks out
I'll sure get it good   on the counter again
         tho my teeth are about to
shake from a creased   shatter like ice waste
         bag in the 70s nightlight
                 in which I never wed

God, I Got Down There to Get Off

Under the lip of the ottoman, something copper winks.

But I'm flat on my belly, hand in my jeans—
and how to say every penny has become the eye
of a dead relative watching me? This one is from 1989—

I'm tapping my 6th-grade self on the shoulder,
watching her turn around with a sneer
(the boy behind her is like, *what?* I didn't even *touch* you that time!)

quispiam est vigilo: is this how the dead continue to watch?

In this compromising position, prone, missionary, firearm—
my lower lip fat with guilt, I think grief delights
in catching me at all the wrong angles though I know
it stares without judgment, with an animal's open fixity.

The metal eye records me dark along the carpet—
regards me in some carbonless curiosity
though, for a divot of time, I do the deed furtive,
without pleasure, but how to say I'm a thing with eight eyes
& there is no thing on earth I want *[them I want them I want them]*.

Knocked slant, high pitched, I am filled with a quiet voracity
& finish the thing I got down there to do
with the same corkscrew intensity, same jacked-up copper wings.

When I Came to There Was a Pearl and a Fish Hook

in my palm where there used to be an earring
I need some air I said   a lie
because I went out back by the sand box   it looked like a turtle
where the air didn't move   his shell was missing
and he was muddy inside   there was a pickaxe
and there were mosquito eggs   hatching inside him

I sat right down under the window unit though
it was pointing the wrong way   dripping cool water
on my neck and arms   I got real thirsty
then something moved in the sun tea jar   I'd been brewing
for the past month   the thing stared out
it put a jelly fist against the glass   it had 4 finger buds

I swore then it got cloudy and I couldn't see it
I popped some fallen juniper berries between my toes
I put some in my bra   nobody knows
but later on I put all those berries the pearl and fish hook
under the tires of my neighbor's Corvair I hid in a hedge
and waited for him to go to work   at the hospital

he pulled out and it didn't make much sound
but when I couldn't see his car anymore I put my nose

right down next to that blue smear
I got real high but the pearl was gone
the hook was still there
through the stuff like gin I went inside

and breathed in
I don't know how
I moved my hands
to make myself a baby

It Wasn't Phenomenal, She Followed the Phone Poles Up & Up

she just kept walking
til it wasn't so choke and violet
to weird her the farmhouse didn't have a phone
her father said he'd leave a light on but he left 2
      the 2nd was dim from the loft of the barn
            at night the road was something softer
                  she couldn't stop following it
          tho the church's cross stood up like the mast
              of a ship half-sunk in the side of a hill
         tho someone hunkered downwind a few yards
      off the road said there are a thousand green lights up there
    if you can stand the bramble if you can stand that fog it'll bite you
like a kerchief full of ether when the phone rings

Lucifer Who Put This Moment in a Clear Block of Gelatin

Lucifer who preserves to what end this odorless black snap:
almost too dim to see the diorama
1971—my grandmother in a moss green sundress
one leg in the bathtub, one out. I can make out
her negative edges, the bubble cup curls which bloom
      in small skeletal fleurs—only half in the world
         she is bending down, smiling over a stroked fly
      something small, dropped inside the drain, I cannot see
the sickness, the three seconds that will snap her
down like a switch, *there*
her vision cracks like I'll always be
the thing nascent, esophageal
      caught mid-gargle in the black—
         rust-flecked egg phosphorescent,
radioactive fish which makes its own light with, *oh*
      a half-life of something so much longer than her stopped
olive toes, less porous than the thing I know *could* be
      and she only half in the shell of this time
      an aneurysm opens its trap, or the devil says:
you will never know her, you never even happened

The Woman Who Stepped From the Black Lincoln

moved like my grandmother but the way she extended her foot

bones rowing—a delicate mannequin ankle borne into summer

lording it over the corn and manure—I had no time for dressing

she rose up in the dust storm eccentric from her eye-slick coffin

and greeted my mother like she'd just lost her load at St. Anne's

when I went to welcome her home she cut me short with a word

"Sorry" her hand cool as cheesecloth it brushed my dirty sternum

she said "I don't think I know you, no, we were never introduced"

what I saw wither back in the chrome tailpipe wasn't an invitation

Erin with the Feathered Hair

She is standing in my living room
straddling her brother's outgrown Huffy:
she wants me back in the cul-de-sac badlands.
Hair freshly feathered, she is showing off
her air-conditioned underwear, a Weiner's six-pack,
stolen margarita lip-gloss in her snatching hand.
I *know*: it's hot and I never left.
She runs to my closet and cuts all the necks out,
never asked and never will,
would I like a red cigarette?
When no one is looking, I twist in the sheets and—
what do you think? Am I a Roxy Music album cover?
I can iron out my voice, but still
I am field stock, body a rebar.
She yanks my freckles, my towhead out of hiding,
smearing my body in bright orange paint and profanity,
flinging open my cupboards and sneering,
What's in the shoebox? Something bad?
In the summer she unpeels my northern pretense,
leaves me quivering in a glitter tube-top
as she unlocks the liquor cabinet and gives me the keys
to the duplex kingdom she swears is rightfully mine.

Post 11th Birthday, He Leaves the Camera Rolling

The cat ambles in and out of frame.
Someone picks up the camera, sets it down;
the frame jogs twice. Then they're laughing.
They've just discovered: my party was a silent movie
but who's to blame for forgetting to check the volume?
Briefly, they consider calling me back:
rewrap the presents, relight the candles.
No, it's just too silly and I'm not a good enough actress.

They break into the Jack Daniels
he lies about his age more than once, speaks in Cajun French,
shows off his muscles, accuses my mother
of buying him presents that are really for her.
Shot of the wok, shot of the blender, they get drunk.

My voice is faint off-camera: *Coke! Coke!*
My mother slurs back: *Not now, I'm a film director!*
He pretends to cook a roux,
puts a frozen egg-roll in his pants pocket.
My mother goes *ooooohhh, baby*
but in the end, it's my fault—
my incessant demand for cola cuts things short
just as they begin to get interesting.

My mother's hand descends over the camera lens,
a slow-mo jellyfish. He grabs it by the wrist—
it curls up like something stunned.
No, he says, *not like that.*

VISITANT

I have had these sounds—when she was suspended in a swing from the ceiling—when she was enclosed in a wire cage—and when she had fallen fainting on a sofa. I have heard them on a glass harmonicon—I have felt them on my own shoulder and under my own hands. I have heard them on a sheet of paper, held between the fingers by a piece of thread passed through one corner.

The Thing in the Middle Which Has No Corner

and no handle
a sick animal
nose nudged
of apple blossom
oil I couldn't use
a sound dropped
a swarm of seeds
a large grey moth
a hash-marked door
something moved
an old rotary phone
three stump-legged
tumors got under
mine to move then

a tall black something
loitered in the median
against a low bower
its eye ran over with
my hands from above
it was a lead blanket
dragged beneath my shoe
stuck inside my windpipe
flapped back there then
a heavy smell rang like
full in the face and then
sheepdogs covered in
the house which wasn't
by god they moved it

. . . la Parc Darque But You Can Only Magnify It

I just wandered up there
for a moment
a hide mitten sodden
in a high gate
a moment something
where it once
boiled egg lay peeled
it had a cake
already salted there
in the frame
and none could be
anyway you
its topside with 1
eye spotting
life more fully

so many times
& it only fluoresced
the canopy made
stretched, half torn
the leaves stilled
moved in the fence
was warm a hard
under a beech tree
of dirt its topside
were no animals
to snuffle it out
superimposed
could only spot
eye closed, 1
itself in another
exposed

...& the Southern Cross Slid Below the Belt

this was before our time: coals in a jewelbox

                      stars in a coalsack

something flagged it down

                     way down where

this coat of arms not cold out
this crux is not the issue

                     my eye naked

this anchor

                     sinks down south

this treasure trail
this Eureka

Jesus under a cellar of black ice, fixed
underground, under god

by musca
this fly hummed hymn in reverse

                     an egg sac moves, Mary
                     in and out of my reach

underwatch the driftweeds
where it silvers off I cannot stop it

this downward dog
this pole position

a Chevy rolls under the canal's heavy wrists

a crucifix dangled upward from its rearview

Somebody Shook Me: Wake Up It's Raining Oil

or it looks like oil sheeting   down the window patience   I don't think it has a smell

& it's stained the glass gray   I'm afraid you must come   downstairs to see be careful

every step's turned on flesh   & the handrail's slathered in   apricot jelly baby if only we

bought you the plastic pool   or had a birdbath or an old   washbin now who will ever

believe we struck it or were   stricken o I'm sorry I forgot   to pay the electricity can I

make you some fried eggs?   just pretend they're not raw   o my patience is starting to

melt you see?   I started to   open the window somebody   shook & shook me I stuck

my tongue out laid it along   the sill she said you'll kill us   that's not your oil to steal

I said it's ink mama not oil   she said you'll kill yourself   that's not your ink to steal

"Would You Like Me to Walk Your Baby?"

I said to the couple on the airplane.
Don't worry; I won't drop him. I'm a dancer;
I never drop anything. Besides, I'm good with babies;
                    I have big breasts & big eyes.
He's just having a little altitude earache. I'll bounce him
on my huge breasts and sing something under my breath.
We'll just take a little stroll down the aisle;
let you two get some shut-eye.
Sure, it's narrow, but so am I.
                    I have no hips to speak of.
Give me your baby, I said with my widening smile,
my enormous breasts, and my pointy pointy shoes.

At the Far End of the Room Buzzed with 40 Tiny Fans

a single beam lights
her hand lowering a bunkmate's into a pan of warm water

on a county road
next to an old service station a woman sits cross-legged beneath

a single pair of headlights
snaking the hill is some girl's freedom to eat, drink, fuck

a VW, the father's feet stop
next to the tire—he bends down and looks under the carriage

she can't get her feet
inside the bed, a pair of panties in the trashcan

just below the dripping radiator
of the stalled bus, a woman with pointy teeth, and she plays

they're so bloody that
no one will claim them and no one will empty the trash

something like a dulcimer
only it isn't a dulcimer, it's the bones of his 9 year-old daughter

a fist-sized scorpion scuttles
down a beam and thuds softly on her floral bedspread

newly clean as flutes'
marrow gone, see the things were musical, the metal diesel sign

and the smell of piss
flowers up in the graffiti code of the cedar rafters

squeaked in the wind
he saw her pointy teeth and ran on fumes for days

To Be Curled in that Snail Light of Your Heathen

friend's panties   the glow worm   man stuck
     'gainst your ribs   & tumbling in   ectoplastic
joy the risk of   sleeping under   her canopy's
     sticker galaxy   phosphorescing   or marigold
butter blooms   which just exist   on packaged
     panty sets &   if there's no fan   & if she pees
in a glass &   says chamomile   tea do you sip
     if she covers   your mouth with   her crotch
do you dare   to inhale what   she keeps in her
     ballet tote   'sides 2 shoes   rights a wrong
smelling of   cider & unwashed   birds her face
     a collapsed   pear as some half   sister brushes
her hair &   she curdles it's time   you go home

The Nursery with Half a Window Up Near the Ceiling

The church was far too old to have its children stuck down
in the mudded foot like that—
the hallway was two feet wide, smelled of Sanka on a Bible
discrete spit seeping the doll-
heads in this basement where
they put the singles, the bell choir, and the Christmas crèche
The electricity went out but
there was no storm, the news said this man was on the loose
The ritalin girls who watched
the babies said *rape* then they
all started to cry, their fat flesh quivering in jeans: *Jesus…*
A man leaned down to look in
the half-window but we could only see his boots pointing in
"He might like big girls or little
girls & even the iron bars won't
block his penis if he wants in bad enough" they said, and then
they stuffed the boy babies under
the crib and the girl babies down in the diaper pail with a prayer

They Shared Her on a Chicken White Sheet

and called her erin

winter   who once was a soprano II

but moved to Minneapolis instead   in spite

                                        of her ankle tattoo

made a sound like filigree in fresh

powder   when they ratcheted her up

to their level and one boy said   you see this?

                                      and the other said

can it dance? what with her whorl

of black   egg hair she's ductile as a shoat

no sleigh of hoarfrost on the swiss   sloped roof

                                      and the sweetest

thing was she wasn't full

of parting shot   and at least they still had her

pom socks to look forward to   that's one thing

                                      about swing dancers

To Step Off the El's Chlamydeous Tongue

and tell your rapist I would like a roast nectarine
    spilled from the rucksack at the mouth of an oak
where every girl is naked & black in the gaslight
        or to compare his close prick to a leaking faucet
or the face of a fingered nickel, or if in the full
          center of the puget sound could he please just
put the plank out, let you step off the ferry's
           clean side unimpeded to say I am nothing but
sonar in february's rimy trench or come tusk
            to tusk with the elephant iced to the bottom
of the sea or the platform you step off in boston
           for the perianth light of this violent
thing you
say you don't want to lick beneath his jackboot

The Amber Thawed, This Black Thing Scuttled Out

they pulled her legs apart
one said he smelled elderberry
one said he saw Vermont

I saw her
she sat on a low-slung Arabian
his white horsehairs fell out
there was only a rubber smudge

I saw them put a pistol under the horse's eye
I heard the crack of skull
someone said it was only the gun
someone said the horse was wooden

I saw wheels on his hooves
she wouldn't get off
they looped a rope around his neck
it came from between her legs
they pulled them both away

he had a squeaky wheel
she had a missing eye
there was something sticky

it was running down the horse
it wasn't blood

the men led on and on
there was no stable
the Indian blanket rubbed a hole in her thigh
the meat was grey inside
one of the men said he smelled burning tire
the other said he smelled karo syrup

she fastened her feet firm in the stirrups
she said oh sorry, oh sorry
with each step her wig kept slipping back
like a doily on the arm of a pink silk couch

Post-Nuptials: The Wedding Party Floated Away on an Iceberg

which was in keeping
the groom wanted to get them alone
they were weaker in isolation

I fell asleep on the train
I had to get up there somehow
I wanted a picture of the bride

before he hung the ice sheet
with her poppy of hymnal blood
right in the center of the floe

when I opened my eyes
I was locked in a black meat box
with a Kodiak bear who salted

my balled body with fake snow
someone had stolen my camera
the train lurched before or after

the bear patted my stomach dry
he said up here the girl who misses
her train is the girl who lives

REVENANT

When the visitant comes again, she is no more a stranger.

The Fox Had No Face the Loggermen Said

they rolled a barrelful of something muffled
down the back of a mountain

a woman moved so fast I couldn't see
what white thing she tucked between her legs

there were spiders hatching inside her mattress
we said that's not what's hatching

she opened her mouth to call her father inside
a small pile of salt fell out

she was wearing a nightdress the color of pistachios
I wanted to throw her over my shoulder

she was too heavy and my arms were marmalade
she pointed to the boulder under the creek

right where the rope swing dropped off
it looked like the skull bone of Paul Bunyan's blue ox

a sudden sickness of red algae bloomed to the surface
the current licked itself clean in a second

Brown Study: A Girl Paces Beneath My Window

ragamuffin, shoeless in the old snow
her eyes over-neotonous in the hedge

this is not my will-be lover's
voice but that of a wry lynx

the enormity of her pockets, little shiv
that makes the epithet slattern so apt

who follows me home hirsute
puts the croup of desire back

she can only gesticulate—doesn't need
words—she has a face, reason to plead

with this whited sepulcher of
my ha, elephantine misogyny

bristles cold in evergreen apostasy, she
lights matches against my foundation

takes off my kid gloves, says
you want but you won't but

a jewel in her drawers, she stalks my sex
where a red deer falls into an iced hole

surrender bears down protean
and inevitable: soft, articulate

A Girl Bellycrawls into My Room in Weeds

she comes like a white bog when I've got my back turned

        but more behind me, down in the floorboards
between that and some dark citrus birdsong
        but from her waist up it's a different story

her hair: never washed, yet always wet and the way it

        rings down louder out la cold orange skirt
but starts in tipping nests, then begins breaking
        up dropping accidental blue eggs on my bed sheet

and when she tries to speak, her tongue gets so speckled

        she can only make one long milk blanched face
I mean she's down under the dust ruffle
        and taps 17 times on my bedpost, which is a wheel

like the thing's a gurney and she's some daguerreotype wet nurse

A Door Left Open at the Place I Didn't Rent

where a carrot colored dog steps down
into the conversation pit I think of Brian
Wilson softening a plug of hashish under
a quarter and how I couldn't figure out
how many stories there were or why it
cost so little for a place with a big pool
though a corner of the tarp was bent up
and the water so thick with sphagnum
it looked like Prell and in that bakelite
shot I said I saw tapeworms swimming
up into the blown summer I tripped on
Lenny Bruce where he was wet & baked
on the Saltillo tile and I thought of a toy
cigarette boat sputtering for fuel when
I flipped my hull I said I can't afford this

We Both Dyed With Feria Starlet,
I Couldn't Dispossess a Girl

and when we got our joint
I panicked: I pictured us in
our nails bit and fertilized:
half moon of my full desire
chemistry: I tried to let her
I got real mean in our house
& kept us stoned out of our
scored from the busboy who
to her senses & pitch 1 for the
go ahead, by all means go get
then she hid my keys so that
started hitting her that night
thin creeks of blood run down
I swear I said *Amie* look what
but how to explain to anyone
me to do it, or blocked exits
acrobatic ways imaginable so
happened until it was done &
in the footed bathtub, cooing
lovely things—why don't you
can't do that? She pried these
finest Hawaiian she could find

florist's license in the mail
overalls, finger-fucking w/
staking a place on the pink
she tried to sway the fixed
sway it with Malibu rum &
she was waitressing then
gourds w/ free shwag she
forever prayed she'd cum
other team & I kept going
some dick: that's my plan
I couldn't go & then I just
and from then on I made
her temples and mouth
you keep making me do!
how she egged & dared
bodily & lied in the most
I was never sure what had
she was washing my hair
what lovely breasts, what
love me? Tell me why you
conversations open with the
& coconut rum, red candles

& at some indeterminate point
my legs like a misplaced bunch
lapping soft as the wading pool
next morning, not talking, just
thin & drawing them back: she

her face appeared between
of romaine lettuce & started
we made a double star inside
plucking our eyebrows razor
w/ her animal sea-green eyes

I Have to Go Back to 1994 and Kill a Girl

It's no wonder

on my belly in

clothing inside
police cars roll

their lights on

they don't see
but I must say

my old house

a book in bed

I'm always tired
It's night & cold

I have to bury her

past but continue
even after shining

I can only assume

1994 is a simpler
I crawl up next to

my mother reads
I want to knock
I need to tell her

with all these tract houses—

the undeveloped field now

a black garbage bag in plot D
down the treeless parkway

me in my freshman sundress

the significance of my presence
time—not everyone is suspect

& look through a lit window

on the glass, there's something

The Woods Are Calling But I Go to a Sleepover

She moves into our old house, finds my diary.

After she burns it, I'm invited to spend the night
but can't find my sleeping bag or my passport.
I *should* be a child but only know word games.

We play in the Dirt Room; her mother brings Fresca.
"*Why*," I ask, "is my old bedroom a turnip plot?
Who's been sharpening their teeth on my trundle bed?"

They're stripping the blonde furniture: *such a bitch*,
& everyone on earth is helping to cook except for me.
There's an ancient training-bra behind the frozen peas.

I'm blindfolded, levitating, they drop me like a 2x4.

In the morning I finally get it: my hair's all gone.
Somebody's chopped it all off, irrevocably;
my friend offers me half her French toast.

I howl to her dad, "do you understand
your daughter symbolically *castrated* me?"

He listens carefully then diagnosis the problem:
"You need a real man, not a boy," he says.

Later he'll wear the hell down & out of me
until I understand the verb *to have,* a teddy.

I Want to Tell Her I Won't Need Calculus, I Want to Warn Her

but she is in the citrine light of her Rosemunde Pilcher

why when her hair is just washed
& nothing really bad is going to happen?

like I wear a ragged cut-out of my yearbook picture

she doesn't question my fear or ardency
but blames it on the drill team

a part of me knocks on the pane, but that's way back

under the black ice of a Kate Bush lyric
I'm so co-o-o-old! Let me in-a-your window

& besides she just fingers the hem of my hiked sundress

when she doesn't know how I'll wear it
alone to the mall with a wall of pink bangs

her body wilts in the gas kiss of her huge humidifier

I really don't mean to scare her but have to
crawdad back & forth on the question

of how much she needs to know to finish her math

I Show Up Twelve Years Late For Curfew

I appear cold, muddy, unstable in the foyer.
My parents are polite, but stiff, like a French host family.

They have new children, who have new toys
which make intergalactic noises in the night.

Their eyes are brown with gold flecks, not like mine.

They either can't remember things or don't care
that I hate tomatoes. Over dinner, my mother asks
my middle name. When I tell her, she says "oh, yes?"

Trying to feel relevant now is a bit like
touching my own mouth shot full of anesthetic,
or forming the word "bouche" while drunk.

I survey the unnatural ocean of their new blue carpet
and try not to chew like a starving person.

This is my family, these people so inept at things like
memory and monopoly, I feel like a trickster god
hiding my funny-money under the board.

I Found Pennies on My Skin, I Put Them There

my bed was covered in copper
I was naked but not smoking
my quilt was cream & smelled like snow peas

I cracked my fortune like a knuckle
my father was still alive
I went to go find him

I found him in Arkansas
someone said he was already dead
wedged under his motorcycle

his girlfriend was my age
she showed me the house
it was on stilts in the middle of nowhere

its white paint was scraped off on one side
it looked like it'd been stolen in the night
somebody said "just a drop in the bucket"

I still had my key
pretended I had been there all along
then the landlord paid me a visit

I met him on the stairs in my bathrobe
pretended to chain smoke
he snuffed my cigarette under his shoe

I closed my robe with one hand
he said "where have you been?"
he looked just like my father

He wouldn't even take my money

He also Outside, a Cold Paisley

below a dark park, he was then
                June under the small rock
                        used on several girls

Should he be the lamb and she like I'm going to come all up in you?

and this is outside
                partial; mindful; dead
                        a black demand sat its rubber smile on the swing

But the old man I told and I forgot something about it

That elegant spit you relax and you hate to close shop

s'why you're the worst kind of girl
                he knocked on the side of the cedar fort
                        and you were like come in there's no door

and when he was finished playing you sealed yourself up the side

like a zipped bag you said I'll give you something to cry about

Glass Backlog

Miniature figurines hold court in my back catalog
Broken ears full of college dictionary obscenities
Chad White is—oh my god—in my bedroom
With his lesser twin, Stephen, and identically
They're touching everything: felled animals
The lemony crotches of shed tights
Quietly, the inhabitants of my Reagan years
Reassume their posts; with every purchase
I'm trying to be better, to upgrade the child's
Garden of verse: a joyful unicorn lurches when I curse
But when I say 'I've changed' I'm full of terror
And here in the realm of all that is *mine*
There are mean boys touching my things

Square in the Gut of Lovemaking Lessons

old elemental roses
fell from the yellow

cracks in the ceiling

A cubic inch of Texas tumbled to the bed

My eyes were still swollen from dusting

Just then, I pinched the blue

bonnet cat-claw of what could be my future, entire

My bed sham shook in its lavender liquidity

My Rangerette boot wanted whitener or death

The AC slowly began
to play Suck & Blow

with the pages of my open book

Briefly, the rhinestone tiara retracted its claws

said, "Fuck me. Go."

A Smoke Ring Lisps Under the Door

When I roll over in bed, I roll over in a California king,
the wallpaper plashed with marigolds in the dark.

You have your fingers inside a little girl.
I cry out, but not for the reasons you think.

The rocking chair that smells of blackened bananas
has an unmistakable occupant now. *You cannot deny me this.*

When you kiss me it is full-cupped, public and flagrant.
You fold your loins into me in recompense for the child
who shimmies away like a little love crocodile.

When the room fills with smoke, a small hand shakes me open.
It doesn't belong to you; you sleep, not animal-like
but thanatopic, a grey shaving of something, once

so sexually resplendent, I barely recognize the skull
which lifts from my grandfather's camphory pillow, the *what is it*
that issues forth, the silvery *fire* in response.

I Invented the Paleolithic Circumstances Beneath This

I chose this peaking bedroom over the barbershop
and this bed, high and flat like an operating table.

I left this note pinned to the sheet and it says
"the stooped man with the grey hat is *your* husband
and this deep-set child came from *your* stomach."

But how when her eyes are boring holes
of need clean through me do I not want her?
Every morning she proffers me flowers in bed.

But the note says "you do not have to answer her
questions or stares. Your husband has given up
his eyes to her and gropes mutely for his shears."

Her eyes are too big for each socket and can see
in the dark. She rubs her swollen egg belly against
the soiled soles of my feet and says *what next?*

Imploring and hungry she waits for me to remember.
Her mouth parts; she intends to ingest me whole.

I leave myself a note pinned to the sheet "You did this."
I did, I invented the ash jibs of this room I cannot leave.

Postcoital Pippi

My lop-eared flesh breathes beside me like a child:

all mouth, tin

type, skin
sticky, but

I deposited

my head in your lap and said:

still, I said

I make my own luck; I *have* to.

You braided my hair and called me your Pippi:

My Pippi!
Silly girl,

you said, you can't ménage a trois *accidentally*—

your old self's a matter

inside you not beside you inside you not beside you inside you not beside you ok? you're not beside yourself.   This is what you said.

But then how do I describe her?   my self, my child cauled

crawled up beside us   this postcoital pippi
            prepubescent possum
panty flowers rising   in buttercup hiccups

            falling   toothless, towheaded
in delicate lavender queefs
                        out of her mind.

Do you *mind?* I said. I put a pillow over her face.

                        Do *you* mind? you said.

NOTES

"You may not realize that you are moving the message indicator, but you are" is part of the Automatism Theory of Ouija at: http://www.museumoftalkingboards.com/theories.html

"I have had these sounds—when she was suspended in a swing from the ceiling—when she was enclosed in a wire cage—and when she had fallen fainting on a sofa. I have heard them on a glass harmonicon—I have felt them on my own shoulder and under my own hands. I have heard them on a sheet of paper, held between the fingers by a piece of thread passed through one corner" is adapted from William Crooke's 1874 essay from the *Quarterly Journal of Science*, "Notes of an Enquiry into the Phenomena called Spiritual during the Years 1870–1873," in which he speaks of the medium Kate Fox's ability to produce raps.

"When the visitant comes again, she is no more a stranger." Adapted from the entry for 'visitant' in the 1828 *Noah Webster's Dictionary of the English Language*.

"I'm so co-o-o-old! Let me in-a-your window" is a lyric from the Kate Bush song "Wuthering Heights" off her 1978 album *The Kick Inside*.

"Not that I'm Neuter Exactly Said the Child in the Yard" was inspired by Louis le Brocquy's *Child in a Yard*, 1953.

"Oh, You Really Don't Want to Go into the Library" was inspired by the 2003 Gus Van Sant film, *Elephant*.

"This Grand Conversation Was Under the Rose" is a response to Jack Yeats' *That Grand Conversation Was Under the Rose*, 1943.

"It Wasn't Phenomenal, She Followed the Phone Poles Up and Up" was inspired by Elizabeth Magill's *Close*, 2000.

"...la Parc Darque But You Can Only Magnify It" was inspired by the 1966 Michelangelo Antonioni film, *Blowup*.

"I Invented the Paleolithic Circumstances Beneath This" is a response to Louis le Brocquy's *A Family*, 1951.

THE AUTHOR

Karyna McGlynn was born and raised in Austin, TX. She holds a BA in Creative Writing from Seattle University and an MFA in Poetry from the University of Michigan, where she received the Zell Postgraduate Fellowship in Poetry and a Hopwood Award. She is the author of several chapbooks including *Scorpionica* (New Michigan Press, 2007), *Alabama Steve* (Destructible Heart Press, 2008) and *Small Shrines* (Cinematheque Press, 2009). Her poems have recently appeared in *Fence, Gulf Coast, Denver Quarterly, Octopus, The Journal, LIT* and *Ninth Letter*. Karyna teaches English literature at Concordia University in Austin, and is currently the Claridge Writer-in-Residence at Illinois College, where she's working on a book-length poem. She edits the online journal *Line*^{4} with Adam Theriault. Her website is www.karynamcglynn.com.